THE SOLO TRAVELER'S HANDBOOK

For those who love and those who long to go solo.

Janice Waugh
aka @SoloTraveler

The Solo Traveler's Handbook: For those who love and those who long to go solo

© Copyright 2011 by Janice Waugh

Library and Archives Canada Cataloguing in Publication

Waugh, Janice, 1957-
    The solo traveler's handbook : for those who love and those who long to go solo / Janice Waugh.

ISBN 978-0-9877061-0-2

1. Travel. 2. Travel--Handbooks, manuals, etc. I. Title.

G151.W38 2011   910.2'02   C2011-904834-5

Disclaimer:

This book provides entertaining and informative snapshots of the writer's personal experiences and helpful tips learned while traveling solo around the world. The tips provided in this book are not meant to serve as a comprehensive checklist to effectively safeguard the reader in every travel situation. The reader should complete updated, detailed research from legitimate sources to learn the cultural norms and safety recommendations for their specific destination. In this day and age, travelers must understand that no one can guarantee safety and that travel can expose them to potential risks. Because safety is impacted by one's actions and choices, the reader is advised to always do their homework on their destination and use their best judgment while on their journey. Safe and happy travels.

For my four sons
of whom I am so very proud.

For my sister, Karen Dale Egan,
who has supported me in countless ways
on the entire Solo Traveler Project.

Acknowledgements

Oh my goodness, how can I thank all the wonderful people who have helped me with this book. My thanks first go to my trusted readers who gently tore my first draft apart. Dale Egan, Elizabeth Verwey, Jeff Jung and Karen Laing, your criticism was so helpful. Then to my proofreaders who saved me from my inclination to miss the details; thank you to Tracey Nesbitt, Judy White Waugh and Jim Egan. To Mariellen Ward, thank you for sharing your self-publishing learning curve and shortening mine. Ana Botelho, thank you for taking my "like this not that" notes and creating a book that matches my vision. Thank you to Joe Yonan, Jim Byers, Marilyn Terrell and Carlo Alcos for taking the time to read and review my book. And, of course, thank you to all the people who supported me through Kickstarter.com and saved me from going into debt on this project. Thank you to my blogger friends - you are the best colleagues I've ever had. Finally, thank you to my sons and my entire extended family who support this book and the entire Solo Traveler project.

Contents

Contents

The Backstory

It was February of 2009 and I was sitting on the couch licking my wounds.

My husband, Ron, had passed away in December 2006 and on that cold Saturday afternoon, over two years later, I felt myself falling into another cycle of grief. But this time, I'd had enough. I got angry. When would it end? And then, for whatever reason, I thought "well, I guess I'm traveling solo".

Ron and I had traveled extensively with our children. We traveled as we could afford - which was not fancy. Early travels included road trips and camping across Canada. We went east to Newfoundland and west to British Columbia. When money became a little more available, we immediately spent it on a six week camping trip through Europe. We knew how to stretch a travel dollar. In 2001/02, after selling our small business, we rented a Volkswagen Pop-up Camper, homeschooled our youngest and traveled Europe for 10 months. Our other sons joined us at various points along the way. We were "The Drifters" with kids.

But in 2009, I no longer had Ron as my travel mate and the kids were grown. With a wanderlust that went back to my pre-teens, I decided that February afternoon that I would travel again as I had in my twenties. I would travel solo.

As a writer with a basic knowledge of the online world, I guess the next step was to be expected. I picked up the computer lying beside me and googled "solo travel". The site I found was full of ads and didn't offer the type of information that I would have found valuable. I decided at that moment to start my blog, Solo Traveler.

The entire Solo Traveler Project - this book, the blog, the Solo Travel Society on Facebook and speaking engagements -- is a personal journey as well as a call to action. I urge you to break the bounds of convention and expectations; to claim the right to be alone, whether for a day or a lifetime; and to travel solo.

At the Mujib Nature Reserve on the Dead Sea - Jordan, 2011

Psyched to Go Solo

While at any given time there are thousands of adventurous travelers discovering the world solo, there are also tens of thousands wondering whether they can. With few exceptions, the answer is yes.

So let's get you psyched

These young dancers attended a school for the arts - Havana, 2005

My Lesson in Havana

I stepped off the plane in Havana at 11:30 pm, passed through immigration and took a taxi into the city. It dropped me in Old Havana, where the street turns into a pedestrian mall. The driver pointed and claimed my hotel was there but, as I looked around, I couldn't see it. The street was deserted. Just me and my carry-on in the dark. Taking a few steps, I heard the sound of my suitcase wheels rolling on the cobblestones echoing off the buildings. I stopped. This didn't feel safe.

But it was no safer standing still, so I moved on. Nothing was lit. I walked right past my hotel until I found a security guard who directed me to backtrack. Walking in the opposite direction I found my hotel and made a mental note: never arrive in a new city after dark.

This was my first solo trip since my twenties. At 49, I didn't think twice about traveling alone. However, my first 24 hours in Havana made me think I should have.

Having found my hotel, I checked in and made it to my room. A room without windows. I sat on the bed and looked at the four walls. The room was clean. The furniture was fine. The bathroom was very nice. It was newly renovated as the travel agent had told me but...no windows? It had not occurred to me to make such a request. I also hadn't thought about arriving in the dark to a deserted pedestrian mall. What else had I not prepared for?

The following morning I asked to be moved to a room with a window, went to a bank and struggled through a currency exchange, ate a terrible meal and got lost in a street pattern that made no sense to me; it was all too much. I returned to my hotel, called my travel agent and requested to be moved to an all-inclusive resort.

By late afternoon the next day I realized that the agent would not be returning my call. I had been politely dismissed. Fortunately, by that time, I was glad. I was enamored with Havana, an old, derelict city that was being lovingly restored.

You see, after I made the call requesting the move, I didn't just sit in my hotel room waiting for a reply. I went for another walk through Old Havana, this time with direction. I headed toward the Capitol Building and enjoyed watching boys playing baseball on the Capitol grounds. They couldn't do that in Washington or Ottawa. I think that was the turning point for me. From there I headed to the waterfront and walked along the Malecón. Then I wandered back through Old Havana exploring; getting lost became a good thing. That evening I ate dinner at my hotel. The food fell somewhere between international cuisine and Cuban. It suited me and helped me relax.

In the end, I was taken by the Cuban culture, so different from home and yet in the same time zone and only three and a half hours away. I was charmed by people who clearly struggled with their country and, at the same time, celebrated it - and rightly so.

My arrival in Havana and moment of panic was simply that, a moment - one I often feel when I arrive in a new city. But, like it did in Havana, the panic always subsides. I learned the lesson of patience on that trip. A lesson that serves me well because it is with patience that the most wonderful adventures begin.

Who is Solo Travel For?

You.

Extroverts:
enjoy time for reflection or take on the world.

Introverts:
gain social confidence or find time to be truly alone.

Singles:
use the freedom you're fortunate to have and meet new people.

Couples:
go individually, grow and invigorate your relationship.

20-somethings:
discover independence.

30-somethings:
figure life out.

Mid-lifers:
rediscover yourself after decades of responsibility.

Seniors:
live a sensational third act.

Everyone:
fulfill your travel dreams.

Why Go Solo?

The Practical Perks

While you may discover solo travel by chance - because you don't have anyone to travel with when you have the time and the money -- you will likely do so again by choice. After all, solo travel is all about you.

- You do what you want when you want. You're on your own schedule.

- You're free to meet locals and other travelers - and, because you're alone, it happens often and easily.

- You're able to focus on the destination and all it offers without distractions.

- You enjoy periods of quiet for reading, art, reflection... you have as much down time as you want.

- You follow your own interests, be they bungee jumping or combing archives.

- You receive special treatment as locals often go out of their way to enhance a solo traveler's experience.

Okay, maybe some of the above can apply to those traveling with a companion as well, but when you travel solo they definitely apply. On a practical level, solo travel frees you to travel your way. But it offers even more.

The Personal Discoveries

Solo travel lets you explore who you are when no one is looking.

At home, family, friends, employers and colleagues influence our actions. Traveling alone, you escape the influence of others and live free to make your own choices.

As you make your choices you learn about yourself - how you like to spend your time, how you feel about things, your personal rhythm.... You get to know yourself better and discover new passions as well as strengths you didn't know you had. Along the way you may collect a few souvenirs like new skills and self-confidence.

— — — — — — — — — — — — — — — — —

"The real voyage of discovery consists not in seeking new landscapes but in having new eyes."

Marcel Proust

The Public Challenge

Solo travel challenges the "single" stigma.

We are a population that is increasingly single. People are getting married later. We are marrying multiple times with periods of singlehood in between. Some choose to be single for life and others find themselves single by loss. With so many singles living full and satisfying lives, why should there be a stigma attached to being so?

Solo travelers defy that stigma one trip at a time. By traveling alone you help redefine the image of the single experience.

"The long-term slide in marriage rates has pushed the proportion of married adults of all ages to 52% in 2009, according to the Census [American Community Survey], the lowest share in history. In 1960, 72.2% of adults over 18 were married."

Conor Dougherty, "New Vow: I Don't Take Thee,"
Wall Street Journal, September 29, 2010.

Solo is the Downward Dog of Travel

Just as the downward dog...

...takes time for the novice to find the position, solo travel requires a bit of time to develop skills to make it both fun and safe.

...stretches and works every aspect of your body, solo travel stretches and works your travel and social skills beyond the typical travel experience.

...is a meditative pose, solo travel gives you real opportunities for meditation and reflection.

...is a rejuvenating stretch, people are rejuvenated by solo travel and return to everyday life with new perspectives.

...is more demanding the longer the pose is held, solo travel can be more challenging the longer one is on the road.

...is a work in progress, the solo traveler is always growing.

No Time Zone. No Jet Lag. Living the FIB Time Warp.

Can we turn back time? Can we live as a twenty-something in our fifties? Can we travel across six time zones without jet lag?

Before my trip to Valencia, Spain for the Benicàssim Music Festival my answer would have been "no". After? Well, let's just say I gained a new sense of the possible.

The FIB – Festival Internacional de Benicàssim – is four days of pop, rock and rap. A huge draw for the Brits as well as the Spanish, this festival taught me that time can lose all meaning. Stimulated by the music as well as the scene, I never felt jet lagged. I survived on very few hours of sleep each night. To bed by 3 am (or 4) and, of course, up early to take in local attractions.

Dancing at the FIB - Benicassim, Spain, 2010

At The FIB, kids screamed. Music pulsed. At times my clothes literally shook from the bass notes. From 6 pm to 6 am, The FIB offered up some of the hottest bands in Europe in a four-day party. This was a press trip and there were other travel and music bloggers there as well. With press passes in hand, we went to the pit in front of the stage to take pictures of the various bands, including Vampire Weekend, The Specials, The Prodigy, Dizzee Rascal, and Gorillaz.

But, of course, I also took off solo to explore The FIB my way.

Wandering to the far stage (there were three), I stood at the back to listen. I had no idea who the band was but they were singing in English and they were great! I made my way towards the front. Then to the very front. I listened to their whole performance. It wasn't long before I was desperate to know who they were but, being considerate of the crowd that was totally with the band, I held back until the end. Then, I turned around and started asking people:

Inglés? Habla inglés?

I found a small group of four who did speak English and told me the story. I was listening to The Sunday Drivers. But this wasn't just any performance of The Sunday Drivers – a wildly popular Spanish band. It was their farewell show. This is why they were the only band I saw that did encores. And, at the end, family and friends poured onto the stage for hugs in celebration. It was a scene.

I had an absolutely fantastic time in Benicàssim. What I learned there was that time is indeed relative – relative to what you are doing. If you're having a great time, the hour, time zones, jet lag...all mean nothing.

Sara Lee has a blog called Live Share Travel. We enjoyed the FIB together - July, 2010

Dream Trips to Real Trips in 7 Steps

If travel is your dream it's important to go.

Don't put things off. You don't know the future so live the present well (with a healthy financial respect for the future, of course). Here are 7 steps, starting with the dream, for great short or long term trips.

1. **Dream.** Dream wildly. The bigger the dream, the better the trip.

2. **Talk.** Tell people about your dreams, what you want to do and why. The more you explain it to others the more real it will become and the better you'll understand why you must go.

3. **Schedule.** Carve out the time that you need. You may only need your regular vacation days or you may need a leave of absence. Be creative and you can negotiate what you require in life. (Oh, did I say life? Of course, I meant travel!)

4. **Save.** Saving for travel is penny-pinching with a huge prize. Read about saving money in the next section.

5. **Research.** Expand your dream by watching films, reading books and blogs about your destination and participating in online forums. You'll discover, through others, just how fantastic your trip can be and learn the practical steps required to make it happen.

6. **Plan.** Bare-bones logistics is all you really need (though I respect those who pull together more). You need to know how you'll get there, where you will stay the first night and how you will manage your money. Beyond that, planning is all about your comfort level.

7. **Go.** Always have your passport ready. Buy your plane/train/bus tickets. Book your accommodation. Go.

Go and enjoy! Don't miss the moment.

Planning and Prepping

Are you psyched for solo travel?

Then get ready to go.

 Meeting people on a beach is easy - Cape Cod, 2010

I Travel Solo for the People

I travel solo to meet people like Skip, Jeanette and Laurie. To learn from people like Jim and Brad. I travel solo for the company I find along the way.

Lunch on the Cape Cod Central Railroad
I started my tour of the Cape on the scenic Cape Cod Central Railroad. Because I was a single, the staff were trying to figure out whether space allowed them to give me a single table. I fixed that quickly. I didn't want to eat alone. I wanted to meet people and I couldn't have met three more interesting, dynamic, opinionated women than Skip, Jeanette and Laurie from Martha's Vineyard.

The energy of each of these women was unique and electrifying. Skip was larger than life. Caution had long been thrown to the wind — she lived life on her terms. Jeanette, though much quieter, was in some ways more adventurous. She had been traveling on her own (and with groups) since her husband passed away in the 90s. Of her upcoming trip to Spain she declared, "I'm looking forward to the tapas bars. That's where the free food is." Laurie, who was the coordinator of this group of 27 women from the Edgartown Council on Aging, had a calm strength. One of her ambitions was to ride a bike across America. Her enthusiasm for her work was obvious.

The four of us talked and laughed. We had the loudest table in the car. We also managed to view the scenery, listen to the commentary and enjoy the fabulous food along the way.

"Are You a Local?"
From the train station in Hyannis I went to the north side of the Cape to Dennis. Driving along route 6A near Brewster, I took a random left and, not surprisingly, found a beach on my first attempt. I wandered a bit and then, curious about the area, I went up to a fellow and asked if he was a local.

The Cape Cod Central Railroad - Cape Cod, Massachusetts, 2010

This is a perfect opening line if you want to chat with someone. If the answer is yes, you'll get insider information on the place. If no, you can ask where they're from. It doesn't matter which direction the conversation takes, one usually ensues.

This is how I met Jim. His answer was no. He was from West Massachusetts and was on the Cape to paint a house. However, he'd been working there a while and it wasn't long before he was telling me about a few highlights in the area including the Ocean Edge Resort and its "million dollar view". We each got in our cars, met there and had margaritas on the terrace. We chatted about life on a large scale and then parted.

Antiquing and Common Histories

After one drink (never more) and before going to the Cape Playhouse that evening, I did a little antiquing. There are many shops and galleries along this section of 6A. At one of them I met Brad. We spoke a bit about his store and the history of it and I soon learned that he was a recent widower. With a shared understanding of loss, we sat and chatted for quite a while.

What a fantastic day. I don't always meet people at this pace when I travel solo but it happens often enough to say that I travel solo for the people.

Tips: Take 'em or Toss 'em

As I write this book, I am trying to cover all possible scenarios for all potential travel abilities, anxiety levels and destinations. Therefore, the information is detailed and yet, it may not be detailed enough. It's an impossible task.

Some tips will apply in some situations but not in others. Some may not be useful on your next trip but could be very valuable on a future trip. I encourage you to use as many tips as seem right for you and don't worry about leaving the rest behind.

I also encourage you to find your own solutions to solo travel issues and please, share them with me and other solo travelers on the blog (solotravelerblog.com) and the Solo Travel Society on Facebook. I also welcome your emails at info@solotravelerblog.com.

Always, use your best judgment. I do.

Make Solo Your MO

Let's put it on the table: people have concerns about traveling solo. I'll admit it: I have concerns at times as well. But I plan and I give myself time at every new destination to settle in and feel comfortable. And then, the most wonderful travel experiences ensue.

People tell me that:

- Traveling alone doesn't feel safe.
- Dining alone is awkward.
- Traveling alone is lonely.
- Traveling solo I have to be responsible for everything.
- If I go alone:
    - There's no one to share experiences with.
    - There's no one to share memories with.

I understand. I've experienced each of these concerns from time to time. But, in my mind, the pros far outweigh the cons. Thanks to a few tactics I've discovered in my travels, and the people I've met along the way, none of these concerns have warranted any real hesitation about solo travel.

So let's get started. Let's explore how to make solo your MO (your modus operandi).

Money: Meaning and Managing

Money, that piece of paper or plastic in your pocket, has no value until you buy something with it. Then, its value is up to you. Is it:

- One taxi ride or public transit and a latte?
- One week at a resort in high season or a two-week road trip?
- A DSLR camera or a quality point & shoot and good walking shoes?

As a solo traveler, you, based on your values alone, choose how to budget your trip. There is no need to compromise with someone else. You set the budget and you decide when to break it. And break it you will.

The key to breaking the budget successfully is in knowing how to make trades. You can come in under budget one place to break it in another. It's usually quite easy.

On a trip to Santiago, Chile, I paid the equivalent of $35 for my first transfer from the airport to my accommodation. Over the course of my stay, I made that transfer three more times, each time less expensively than the last. In the end, I saved $54.40 by taking transit rather than a taxi. I spent that money on a wonderful piece of textile art for which I had not budgeted. I traded convenient transfers for a piece of art that I'll enjoy for a long time.

Money and Stress
Money is capable of causing stress or relieving it. Spending more than you can afford on a trip will cause stress as you will pay for it when you return. Spending a lot on travel gear, even if you can afford it, can cause stress if you travel worrying about losing the gear. However, spending more money than normal on accommodation in a city where you have safety concerns will reduce stress. Plan your budget with these important issues in mind.

Saving Money for Travel
Some people dream about travel and others do it. It's not that the doers

are independently wealthy, but they know how to save. Here are some tips to get you needed travel dollars:

- Define your dream destination. Put a photo of it on your fridge or your screen saver. Keep it top of mind and then weigh every purchase against that dream.
- Set up an automatic withdrawal from your regular bank account and send the money to a dedicated travel account. Would you miss $20 a week? That adds up to $1040 a year — enough for a single person to do something fun for a week or maybe more depending on your taste.
- Don't think you can afford $20 a week? Make and bring your lunch, go back to regular coffee rather than lattes, walk or cycle rather than drive or take transit. Each of these changes are healthy lifestyle choices and will easily save you more than $20 a week.
- Buy with a credit card that has no annual fee and offers cash back on purchases. Pay the card off in full every month and don't shop at more expensive stores just to get the reimbursement. Add your cash back to your travel fund.
- Use the library to cut your entertainment costs by borrowing books and DVDs.
- Hold potluck dinners rather than entertaining people.
- Drop your long distance package from your phone bill and use Skype. It may even make sense to eliminate your home phone completely.
- Dine out at lunch rather than dinner — especially at fine restaurants. The quality will be the same but the cost will be much lower.
- Know how you react in an impulse buy situation. Some people are stopped by seeing cash leave their hands, others by the prospect of using a credit card. Carry whichever form of money you are less likely to use.
- In the same vein, have a "spend no change" policy. It will add up nicely in a jar - especially true in Canada where there are $1 and $2 coins.
- Sell your unneeded stuff online. It's amazing what you can sell and it will be cash right into your pocket. Sell many things at once to be efficient with your time.
- Write down everything you spend. Just knowing how much you're spending and where, will help you save.

I'm sure that you can come up with your own ways to save travel money.

Money and Points

With all the rewards programs available, it is possible to travel a lot while spending only a little. People who do this really well are called Travel Hackers. Look at the resources at the end of the money section for links on travel hacking.

Steve from Seattle Serves Me Starbucks in Patagonia

My ultimate destination for my trip to Chile was The Towers in Torres del Paine, Patagonia. It's the grand prize for the average hiker. At the lookout for The Towers, I met Steve – another solo traveler.

Steve was more than the average hiker. He had just completed the entire Torres del Paine circuit, which is a nine-day challenge. An airline pilot on forced sabbatical (layoff), this was one of the many trips he was getting in before being called back to work.

After visiting The Towers, I descended to the beginning of the trail and took the shuttle bus to the main road where I had a two hour wait for the main bus. I had noticed a coffee shop there before taking the shuttle into the trail and was looking forward to a hot cup of coffee (good or bad) while waiting.

Unfortunately, the coffee shop was abandoned.

Fortunately, I met Steve again.

A couple of hours wait gives solo travelers time to get to know one another. The conversation rambled. We exchanged stories. Steve, as it turned out, was from Seattle. And, when he learned that I had been hoping for a coffee, he took a packet of Starbucks instant out of his backpack. But of course.

He then took out his stove, boiled up some water and served me a coffee.

Thanks to Steve and all the travelers, solo and otherwise, who help each other on the road.

Hamming it up a bit, but truly, Steve's coffee was a treat -
Torres del Paine National Park, Chile, 2011

Spending Money - Setting a Budget

Whether you're established financially or a struggling student, at some point you need to decide what your trip will cost and if you can afford it. This is where reality challenges your dreams and your bank account is the judge.

The easiest way to budget your trip is to look at the cost of getting to your destination first and then add your daily expenses. Determining your daily expenses may be difficult to do online. This is where the travel guides such as Lonely Planet and Frommer's excel. As a person with far too many travel guides that are out of date, I suggest that you borrow one from the library.

In your daily expenses you need to consider:

Accommodation: Whether you'll stay at hostels or expensive hotels, these costs are relatively easy to determine.

Food: You don't want to live on porridge for days at a time (I met one traveler who did) but you don't need fine restaurants every day either. Determine what you want to spend daily knowing that you will spend more on some days and less on others.

Transportation: Local transportation varies greatly. Cabs may make sense in some cities but be an unnecessary expense in others.

Entertainment: From wine tours to museum visits to theater, you need to anticipate approximately how much you will spend.

Multiply your average daily expenses by the number of days you'll be at your destination, add your cost of getting there and you'll have an approximate budget.

Drawing up a budget doesn't have much value unless you stick to it, so track your expenses daily. This can be on your laptop, your smartphone or in your journal. What matters is that you know where you stand regarding your budget. It can make the difference between returning with regrets or a fabulous souvenir you didn't realize you could afford.

Handling Money on the Road

Carrying cash and paying for things is an issue for solo travelers. You alone are responsible for doing both safely. You have a number of options:

- Debit cards which access your bank account directly.
- Credit cards which build up debt for when you return.
- Prepaid credit cards or products like a Thomas Cook Cash Passport. You load the card with the amount of money you want available.
- Traveler's checks which you purchase at your bank. They are no longer common but they do exist. To cash them you will likely have to go to a bank or chain hotel. Stores may not accept them.
- Cash. It's good to be able to pay in the local currency as you will get better prices.

All of these options include transaction fees of various sorts. Check with your financial institution to understand them. When possible, use local ATMs rather than currency exchange counters in airports and train terminals, as these tend to be more expensive.

To minimize complications when you travel:

- Have more than one means of getting cash such as a debit card and traveler's checks or two debit cards that use different international systems.
- Have more than one credit card with you. It's a good idea to have a Visa card since they are so widely accepted.
- Call your credit card companies before you go to let them know where you're traveling and for how long.
- Keep half of your financial resources in your money belt or room safe.
- Don't carry more money on you than you think necessary and keep it in two locations, for example, a pocket and a purse. Men, don't keep your wallet in your back pocket.

- Have the telephone numbers of your credit card companies and banks with your travel paperwork so that you can call them immediately if you lose your cards.
- Consider how you will top up a prepaid credit card or move cash around when traveling. Using public Wi-Fi is not advisable for this purpose. If you are visiting friends along the way, plan to use their secure Internet. In a pinch, I have requested and been granted access to the Internet at a bank.
- Consider the cost of each system when deciding which you will use. If you travel a lot you may want to have a premium account that allows international withdrawals for a flat fee.

Great resources:

BudgetYourTrip.com - this blog has basic cost information on a variety of locations and suggests what your daily expenses will be.

ThePointsGuy.com - this site and blog direct you to great deals for all the major loyalty programs and describes how to best use your points.

TravelHacking.org - a service that you pay for on a monthly basis that helps you win in the world of travel hacking. This is run by Chris Guillebeau of The Art of Nonconformity fame.

Xpenser.com - offers an expense tracker and management tool that works from just about any device.

Ditching the Digital World

I'm online almost all the time.

My writing practice, my blog, social networking… they are all demanding and I sometimes wonder what I'm missing by not giving my mind enough wander time. This is why I implemented my annual Digital Detox a few years ago. Every autumn I go offline completely for as many days as I can afford. In '09 I spent four days offline in the Lake District.

The Lake District has a romantic past. William Wordsworth and the Lake Poets drew attention to this special area in the Northwest corner of England during the 19th century. It has since become a destination for nature lovers and walking enthusiasts everywhere. With no history as a hiker, off I went.

I discovered that there is something strangely addictive about walking the hills, or fells, as they are called locally. On my first day I spent almost 4 hours covering a mere 10k. After a couple of hours walking it appeared that I had reached the top so I took photos of my success. As I continued along the path to descend, I discovered that I had to go up some more. I did half of the walk in the rain and all of it walking through water. Drenched and a bit frustrated I wondered: is this fun? Do I like this? Is the notion of walking better than the actual doing? Yet, I awoke the next day eager to go out again.

As the saying goes, "there is no bad weather, only bad clothing". So, taking full responsibility for my wet feet of day one, I bought a pair of waterproof hiking boots the next morning and set out again.

It was a wise investment. It rained numerous times every day I was there and the paths I walked were often streams; that's why there are lakes.

My destination on day two was Grasmere via the Coffin Walk, the path along which people from Ambleside carried their dead to a consecrated

The fells were beautiful in all directions - Lake District, England, 2009

Some of the paths were a bit more demanding than the term 'walking' would suggest. This is a vertical climb - Lake District, 2009.

burial ground in the 19th century. By the time I reached the lovely Rydal Tearoom, not a quarter of the way to Grasmere, I was drenched again - except for my feet of course.

I hung my jacket near the high efficiency fireplace, ordered a pot of tea and sat down on a comfortable couch. Soon two men sat on the couch opposite and, as is usual for me, I started a conversation. It wasn't long before we set off together towards Grasmere. Chris and Peter of Liverpool were wonderful company. They gave me a history of the fells and pointed out details of the flora and architecture in the few small cottages we passed that I would never have noticed had I made the trip alone.

I hiked one more day up the pike of Wansfell. Unfortunately, it was in a cloud when I got there. But, later in the day, on my descent, I had a wonderful view of Lake Windermere. When I saw the panorama that I had thought would elude me that day, the views I had enjoyed, the pleasure of physical exertion, the satisfaction of having walked for three days straight, all converged and I was in love. The Lakes now hold a truly special place in my heart.

As for my digital detox, there were no shakes, no anxious moments. Walking requires focus. It demanded my attention to get my footing right, to follow the map and instructions, to stay on course and to take in the beauty. It was easy to leave thoughts of work behind. Ditching the digital world can be done, especially when walking the fells.

Where to Lay your Head

For the typical traveler, accommodation is a matter of taste and budget. For the solo traveler, it is much more. Your choice of accommodation will affect your travel experience greatly. Here are options and what you can expect.

B & Bs

Bed & Breakfasts (or Tourist Homes as they are sometimes called) are located in private homes and typically more expensive than hostels but less expensive than hotels. A bedroom, shared or private bath and breakfast are offered. There is usually a sitting room to be shared by the guests and a communal table for breakfast, making this style of accommodation ideal for solo travelers. You are on your own for all other meals of the day.

B & B owners are usually very friendly and a great source of information on their town or city. Many B & B owners belong to an association and there are a number of rating services online but no standard that is widely used around the world. Luxury B & Bs certainly exist but so do very undesirable ones. Check the reviews and choose carefully.

Hostels

Hostels are great for those on a tight budget and interested in meeting people. Hostels are very sociable and offer basic accommodation, often limited to dormitories and bunk beds, at a low cost. In some cases, private and semi-private rooms are available. Breakfast and free Wi-Fi are often included in the price, as well as access to a kitchen to cook for yourself.

You may think that hostels are for young people only, but they welcome people of all ages and are seeing more in their 40s, 50s and 60s than in the past.

Chicago has an excellent, free Greeters progam. It's great for solo travelers - 2009

Hostels are great places to meet people and exchange information. Travelers learn from each other at hostels. They'll share tips and their favorite places to go, what they thought was worth the time or money and what wasn't.

Some hostels are members of Hostelling International and some are private. The latter are often referred to as Backpackers' Hostels.

Hotels
You don't have to look far to confirm that hotels range greatly in quality. The hotel star system is intended to give you a sense of the quality of a hotel; the more stars, the better the hotel in terms of the amenities it offers.

Unfortunately, the star system varies greatly. North America works on a five star system while Europe works on a four star system. Go to other continents and the system will change again. A five star resort may compare to your understanding of a three star. The star system also focuses on amenities, not charm. Unless you're dealing with a major chain, the star system has limited value and you'll have to do your homework.

Hotels tend to be less social than other options but they usually have trustworthy people with local knowledge to answer your questions.

Apartment Rentals
Renting an apartment is a great way to connect with a community while traveling. Rentals usually start at one week but can run for a number of months. Their cost varies greatly based on size and location. They are usually well equipped. The downside of rentals is that they don't have a social aspect built in like hostels and B & Bs, nor do they have someone at the front desk to answer questions like hotels do. On the other hand, you can go to the same bakery, fruit and vegetable shop and cafe daily and become known in the community. Full payment may be required in advance either by credit card or, in some places, in cash.

Couchsurfing

Couchsurfing is a relatively new phenomenon. Like a B & B, you will be staying in someone's home. You may get a bed or a couch but, in this case, they won't charge you.

Register on a site like couchsurfing.org to get connected to other couchsurfers and hosts. Add as much detail as possible to your profile and participate in the community online and off.

Be cautious with couchsurfing. Look at a prospective host's references, whether they've been vouched for and for their response rate as indicators of how trustworthy they are. Check the "couch" information field to confirm what kind of accommodation you'll get. Message a person you'd like to surf with and carry on a conversation to get a feel for who they are. Consider meeting your prospective host for a coffee before staying at their place.

I'd like to thank Carlo Alcos, a couchsurfing enthusiast and publisher of Vagabonderz.com for this information. It is a condensed version of a complete article he wrote for Solo Traveler called "Overcome Your Fear: How to practice safe couchsurfing."

Others

There are many other options when it comes to accommodation. Though I have not used these personally, I have heard great reports from people who have house-swapped, and stayed in monasteries and university dormitories.

Great resources:

AirBnB.com - As they say: Rent nightly from real people in 13,173 cities in 181 countries. Those numbers change regularly.

BedandBreakfast.com: An online booking engine for B & Bs.

BedBugRegistry.com - The Bed Bug Registry is a free, public database of user-submitted bed bug reports from across the United States and Canada.

Couchsurfing.org - An online community and booking tool for couchsurfing.

Google Street View - http://maps.google.com/help/maps/streetview/ A good tool for checking out the neighborhood of your accommodation.

HomeAway.com - Vacation rentals worldwide.

TripAdvisor.com - Traveler's reviews of accommodation, resorts and more. Take these with a grain of salt as they can be skewed by entries from the company being reviewed.

WomenWelcomeWomen.org.uk - 5W is a network of about 2,400 women in over 80 countries ready to help other women with their travels.

Confession of a Solo BoBo

I suspected it when I traveled solo down the Blues Highway staying at beautiful four and five star hotels yet visiting some pretty seedy bars. It was confirmed when a thrill ran up and down my spine as I bought a backpack for my trip to Chile.

I am a BoBo – a Bourgeois/Bohemian.

I'm middle aged. I'm middle class. I like a few luxuries. But I also like to believe that there is a bit of the Bohemian in me that can discard the trappings of a middle-middle existence and take pleasure in whatever is presented.

Bohemians are often described as wanderers or adventurers. I'm happy to claim those labels.

At home I can be somewhat traditional, dare I say Bourgeois. But when I travel, I like to take a less conventional approach. Someday I may raise this approach to an art form and maybe even live it full time.

Until then, I am a BoBo.

Feeling small in Torres del Paine National Park - Patagonia, Chile, 2011 ✈

Packing: You Are Your Own Sherpa

I know. A carry-on? Some people can't do it, but in my opinion, it's a must. I can't emphasize enough just how beneficial it is to pack lightly. Whether you use a suitcase or a backpack, conforming to carry-on standards has many advantages:

- Quick electronic check-in.
- No wait at the luggage carousel.
- Easy transfers between planes and terminals.
- Local transit to airports is an option.
- No need for help at your hotel, hostel, B & B...
- Your luggage won't be lost by the airlines.

And...

- You won't fumble with luggage, which makes you a more capable traveler.

But...

- Be considerate. Follow carry-on rules and don't overstuff your items. One item in the overhead and one at your feet is reasonable.

Carry-on or Backpack?
If you are city traveling, a carry-on suitcase is easy to roll along the streets. Adventure travel or travel that involves multiple cities and transfers may be easier with a backpack.

Neither has to be particularly expensive. I spent $40 on my carry-on five years ago and it's taken almost 20 trips with me. My 40 liter backpack is newer and a little more technical. I spent $130 on it and I love it.

Sample Packing List

You don't need to pack much more for a month than you do for a week - if you are strategic.

On my two week trip to England during a rainy November that included hiking in the Lake District and meetings in London, I needed a wide range of clothes and gear. This was my greatest carry-on challenge to date and I will use it to demonstrate how you can pack lightly for a variety of situations.

1. Bulky items

Wear or carry your bulky items. Plan your packing list knowing that you'll wear your bulkiest items on the plane. I wear my bulkiest pants, sweater (with t-shirt underneath) and waterproof rain coat to the airport. I never pack hiking boots. When moving around, I tie them onto my carry-on but at the airport I wear them and pack away my shoes.

2. The essentials

First pack the basics. These go on every trip:
- All paperwork, accommodation confirmations, flight information, itinerary, passport and travel insurance information. Pack duplicate copies of these in another location such as your purse or day pack.
- Global plug adaptor.
- iPod and power connector.
- Book to read, diary and pen.
- Computer and AC adapter.
- Cell phone and charger.
- Camera and charger.
- Vitamins and water bottle.
- Small first aid kit.
- Hair products, face cream, makeup, deodorant, toothbrush, toothpaste.
- Quick-dry microfiber towel.
- A couple of large resealable plastic zipper bags for wet items.
- A few feet of duct tape (amazing what it can be used for).

3. Clothes

To have clothes for a range of activities and look good, choose one color palette. For the UK trip, mine was black and gray with purple as the accent.

- Shoes – one pair street shoes, one pair heels. (wear hiking boots)
- Pants – one pair black dress pants. (wear jeans)
- Tops – one blouse, one light sweater, one camisole (that works as an under layer for hiking and under a jacket for business), colorful t-shirt. (wear casual sweater and t-shirt)
- One cardigan and one light jacket that dress up or down – both work with the cami and t-shirts.
- Belts, scarves and possibly jewelry (small, light and inexpensive) – to dress up casual clothes.
- Umbrella, scarf, gloves, rain pants, hat, vest, sunglasses.
- Pajamas, underwear, socks for four days.

Rinse clothes out when necessary.

To meet the two item carry-on limit, women might want to carry their purse and extra shoes in a light weight nylon bag. This is also great for carrying souvenirs on your return trip if you don't buy much. If, however, you are a shopper, please be courteous of other travelers by not pushing your carry-on limit. Check a bag.

4. Scarf

I have to mention my white cotton pashmina-style scarf. Unless it's winter, it goes everywhere with me and has functioned as a:

- Head cover in religious sites.
- Face protector from wind and sand in the desert.
- Towel.
- Pillow protection in a dodgy hostel.
- Cover-up on the beach.
- Accessory to dress up a simple black shirt.
- And, of course, a scarf for warmth.

The scarf protected me from wind and sand in Wadi Rum - Jordan, 2011. ✈

Don't ruin your fun by...

Opting for fashion over function. If you fuss too much over fashion you will likely end up carrying too much or wearing clothes that are uncomfortable.

Wearing uncomfortable shoes. This is actually the same point as above but, because it's your feet, it needed a separate entry. Nothing will ruin a trip faster than sore feet.

Holding to beauty routines that are unmanageable on the road. It is worth having easy hair options so your travel time is not consumed with such a mundane task as finding a salon for a color.

Arriving in a city in the dark. At night new places can look a little ominous and make you anxious. Don't lose fun time with unnecessary doubts. Arrive during daylight.

Attracting unwanted attention. Expensive jewelry and revealing clothing can inadvertently attract attention from the wrong people. Adapt to your location.

Leaving valuables vulnerable. Choose a purse that you carry across your shoulder. Carry it with the opening to your body and keep it zipped. In busy places, carry your daypack on your front and wrap your arm around it. Carry a money belt or use the hotel safe. Protect your valuables at all times.

Avoiding Culture Shock

The novelty of a new country is one of the great joys of travel - or the cause of serious culture shock.

It can be stressful when you don't know the language, exhausting when you can't accomplish the simplest of tasks and frustrating to be socially clumsy because you don't understand the culture. Here are a few tips to help you minimize the impact of culture shock.

Be knowledgeable: Research before you go. Read what you can, including blogs, newspapers or novels from your destination.

Be connected: Ask friends and family for a local contact. It's wonderful to receive a personal introduction to a new culture when you travel alone.

Be comfortable: Pack carefully to ensure that you have the appropriate clothes for your destination. You will feel more comfortable if you are properly dressed.

Be a chameleon: Watch carefully how people greet each other, whether they line up for a bus, how they buy fruit... there are nuances in every aspect of a society. Look for them.

Be appropriately social: Observe how people interact in groups large and small, including where they stand, how they speak, where their eyes land...

Be respectful: Follow local customs to blend in and stay out of difficult situations.

Be oriented: Start your visit with an overview of the city by taking a local tour. A walking tour will give you a close-up look at the culture but bus tours can be helpful for the bigger picture.

Be supported: Befriend your hotel desk clerk or coffee shop owner – anyone who you see on a regular basis and can become your local go-to person for questions.

Be patient: If you are feeling culture shock, find a quiet place to relax and regroup.

(This was written by my son, Dylan who does stand-up comedy on occasion. He just rattled these off.)

15 Signs that You've Had Too Much Alone Time

1... You've gone about as far as you can learning to play the harmonica.

2... You've worn the same shirt across 3 borders but think: "well, it's new to them."

3... You step into a cab and "that smell" Is you.

4... Your internal dialogue becomes your external dialogue.

5... Fingers become appropriate utensils for just about any occasion.

6... When you find an engaging conversation, the only response you can muster is "uh-huh".

7... You spend more than 20 minutes talking to your mugger – and he doesn't speak English.

8... You catch a fish and find yourself just petting it.

9... Calling cards become a major budgetary item.

10... You pretend to be lost just to talk to someone.

11... You see Sudoku when you close your eyes.

12... You sleep in your clothes.

13... You go to the hotel lobby in your pj's.

14... When you speak you only vaguely recognize your own voice.

15... You're so desperate to communicate in some way that you write a blog called Solo Traveler. (This one was for me.)

Solo in a Group

Though I'm typically an independent solo traveler, I would like to dedicate some attention to groups for solo travelers. It can be the right choice for some people all of the time and for others some of the time.

The Pros and Cons of Packaged Travel
Solo travel can mean joining a group but not knowing anyone before you go. You might love this option. Here are the pros and cons:

Pros:

- The planning is done for you, including all the logistics and hotel bookings.
- Language and cultural barriers are handled for you.
- You are sure to see the major sites.
- If things go wrong, someone else is responsible for setting them right.
- There is safety in numbers.
- You know that you'll have travel companions.
- You won't ever have to eat alone.

Cons:

- You may have to pay a single supplement (more on this soon).
- You will typically meet fewer locals and have fewer surprises (of the good kind).
- You may not see things off the beaten track.
- You can't save money on things that aren't important to you and splurge on things that are.
- You may be stuck with people you don't enjoy.
- You don't control your schedule.

Selecting the Tour That's Right for You

Whether your interest is adventure, culture, history, volunteering, shopping or walking... you'll find a tour company that fits your budget. But how do you decide which company is for you? Here are some guidelines:

- Review the itinerary carefully and compare it with other itineraries for the same destination - even those out of your price range. Once you know all the options, you'll be able to choose the tour that's right for you.
- Take note of what is and isn't included in the price, from transfers to meals. You want to know that you have enough money to really enjoy the trip.
- Know their refund policy.
- Look at the demographics of the group. Is this the group you want to travel with?
- Find out how large the group will be. Does this suit you?
- Is there a single supplement? Will they pair you with another traveler to avoid the single supplement? Can you negotiate away the single supplement?
- Consider the reputation of the company. Look for reviews of the tour but also check with friends and use Facebook and Twitter to get firsthand feedback on the tour you're considering.
- Talk directly to the tour company to learn:
  - How the company is structured and whether they have people on the ground at your destination.
  - Whether the company is licensed to operate in your destination country.
  - How they choose their guides, what training the guides have and how they are accredited.
  - Their policies around sustainable tourism and buying local.

Wandering on a steamy Sunday, I tripped over this "happening" in Washington Square Park. People, fully dressed, or stripped down had taken over the fountain - New York City, 2010

Beating the Single Supplement

The single supplement is the bane of solo travelers who prefer a tour, a cruise or a resort over independent travel. The idea of paying more because you're only half of a couple seems counterintuitive and is frustrating, but it is an economic reality. Here are a few strategies to beat it.

Google Alerts: When you start dreaming about a trip, create a Google Alert for your destination of choice and the term "single supplement waived". For example: "Caribbean resort single supplement waived". When a notice that the single supplement is waived at a Caribbean resort goes up on the web, you'll receive an email alert from Google.

Ask: Speak directly with the tour company or use a travel agent who will go to bat for you. Either way, ask for the single supplement to be waived. Book your package far ahead of your departure date or at the last minute. The company may be willing to waive the supplement to kick off sales or sell off remaining spots. Of course, it helps if you're willing to walk away from the deal if you don't get what you want.

Pairing Up: Some tour companies will waive the single supplement if you're willing to share accommodation with another person of the same gender.

Find a Travel Partner: If your preferred travel company doesn't offer a pairing service, you may find a travel partner through friends, Facebook or one of many specialty sites on the web.

Simply google "find a travel partner" and you'll find many options. But don't go with just anyone. Be picky about who you'll spend your travel time with.

Go on the Shoulder Season: The off-season is usually "off" for a reason, but the shoulder season can be a spectacular time to travel. With fewer crowds it can be more enjoyable and you may be more successful in negotiating away the single supplement.

Find a Deal so Great...: If you find a screaming deal it just may be worth swallowing your solo pride and paying the single supplement.

Negotiate an Upgrade: If you have to pay the full single supplement, maybe you can negotiate an upgrade on your room or what's included. It's always worth a try.

Let the Adventure Begin

When you travel alone anything can happen.

You're open to the world. And the world is open to you.

Kissed By the Blues

Like a kiss, the Blues can be gentle and sweet or wild and passionate. On my trip down Highway 61, the Blues Highway, I was kissed both ways by the Blues.

What do I know about the Blues? Not a whole lot. I know the majors like Sonny Terry & Brownie McGhee – my brother introduced me to them as a teenager. Buddy Guy – my husband and I saw him in Atlanta. And of course, B.B. King – he actually did kiss me. But that part of the story comes later.

The fact is, I don't know a lot but, when it comes to the Blues, you don't need to know it; you just need to feel it.

Life in 12 Bars
This trip had a Blues theme. After all, I started in Chicago and traveled to New Orleans visiting as many Blues bars as I could. I had wanted to take this trip for many years.

Why? I kept asking myself this question. The only answer I could muster is that there is a magical quality to the Blues. A mythology around its origins. A simplicity that invites anyone interested to enter and enjoy.

And just like the Blues' 12 bar progression has a certain predictability, so does life. And as the tunes share common themes, so do we all. We all live, love, grieve, experience joy and heartbreak. I don't know any other form of music so pure. I guess I was looking for the heart of the Blues.

Solo is not Blue
Many of the people I met on this trip were surprised by my choice to travel solo. They thought I might be lonely and sad. But I wasn't.

I've been those things. I've been blue but not due to traveling alone.

The famous Beale Street. - Memphis, Tennessee, 2009.

As I traveled down the Blues Highway, I sought out the best Blues I could find. Eddie Shaw at Kingston Mines in Chicago and the house band at B.B. King's in Memphis were great. I really enjoyed Jeff Greenberg at Jimbeaux's in New Orleans. But for me, the best was in Jackson, Mississippi at 930 Blues Café. There I thrilled to Jackson's Blues Sweetheart, Jackie Bell – a stunning singer and an equally amazing performer – and all Blues.

At 930 Blues I met Herbert, Isaac the club owner, and Marvin who worked security. As a single woman, I felt wonderfully safe and happy that night. Even as I stepped into the cab to go back to my hotel, Marvin looked the driver right in the eye and said: "you take care of my friend, y'hear." Safe. Totally safe.

Then There's B.B., the King of the Blues

I guess I really fell in love with the Blues the night I went to a small club under the boardwalk in Redondo Beach, California. That boardwalk, along with the club, is long gone but not my memory of seeing B.B. there. The venue was small and somewhat sophisticated as I remember. Cabaret style. B.B. played long sets. At one point a string broke on his guitar and he continued to play as he restrung it. And, later in the evening, he offered the women pins of his famed guitar Lucille.

Shy as I was back then, I was the last woman to make my way forward to get a pin. He looked at me. He had no more. So he leaned in and kissed me on my left cheek.

Oh yes, I've been kissed by the Blues.

The Social Side of Solo Travel

My fondest travel memories are always of the people I meet along the way.

In the solo travel stories peppered throughout this book you meet many of them. Yet, there are countless other people whose company I've enjoyed on my travels - sometimes for a few minutes, sometimes for a few hours. Here are a few of my favorites...

Patagonia, Chile - On the Navimag Ferry on my way to Patagonia to hike in Torres del Paine I met many solo travelers. One was special - Noemie, from France. She has a powerful energy and we struck up an immediate friendship. Within a day we were making plans to camp and hike Patagonia together. She made a magical trip even more so.

Orlando Airport, Florida, USA - On my way to speak at a conference in Florida, I made a whirlwind yet substantial connection with Rick at the Orlando Airport. We exchanged travel stories and life stories. He eventually contributed a post about volunteering on the El Camino de Santiago to Solo Traveler. We continue to stay in touch via email.

Park City, Utah, USA - I first met Olivia on Facebook - we were both going to Park City to volunteer at the Sundance Film Festival. To my surprise, without planning, she was the first person I met when I got there. We kept running into each other. It was extraordinary but not surprising given her great energy and enthusiasm.

Ambleside, Lake District, UK - I met so many people at the Unicorn Inn over the four days I was in Ambleside. It was amazing. On my last evening, when I entered the bar I was greeted like Norm on the television show "Cheers". I couldn't pay for a beer to save my life that night. Such hospitality.

Truly, it's the people I meet who make my travels so wonderful.

Noemie and I met on the Navimag Ferry then hiked and camped together in Torres del Paine National Park - Patagonia, Chile, 2011.

How to Meet Locals and Other Travelers

So how do you connect with such wonderful people as you travel?

- Choose your accommodation wisely. Hostels and B & Bs are naturally more social than hotels.
- Consider traveling by train. The dining, bar and observation cars are great places to meet people.
- Take advantage of volunteer tour organizations like Big Apple Greeters in New York City. You will often find them through the tourist bureau website and many are free. There are also excellent local tour companies in just about every destination possible.
- Learn how to talk to strangers. We'll get to that.
- Take classes to learn a language or new culinary skills - whatever interests you. You'll meet a group of people who share your interest.
- Go to restaurants with communal tables and coffee shops that are freelancer hubs. We'll get to this topic too.
- When you are in one place for a while, go to the same market, flower shop or restaurant consistently. You'll be noticed as a new regular and people will eventually chat with you.
- If you're long term traveling, break up the trip with an organized tour. You'll enjoy the company and a chance to let someone else take charge for a while.

Talking to Strangers

While there are a number of ways to start conversations, the best is your smile. A warm smile tells people that you are friendly and safe. But here are some starters for specific situations:

Locals: Start with a question that allows them to share their love and knowledge of their city or community. Ask about restaurants or the best coffee shop.

Other solo travelers: You'll recognize solo travelers by the place settings at a table or solo seat on a tour. But just because they're alone, don't assume that they want company. Open with something easy like a comment about the weather and see if they take the conversation further.

Other tourists: Chatting with a couple or small group of tourists can be fun too. Look for the person in the group who is gregarious but not the organizer - the latter is too busy being responsible. Just ask where they're from and the conversation has begun.

In a club: Sit at the bar. This is more social than a table. Comment on the band and ask about the music scene in town. It will be obvious that you are a tourist, which makes you interesting.

Anywhere: If you are really, really curious about something, spot a person you'd like to speak with and ask your question. There is nothing better than genuine curiosity to engage people.

Master the art of the follow-up question. Ask "why" and "how" questions that are open-ended. People love talking about their city, themselves, their thoughts and knowledge.

"Tell Me Your Story"
When it is clear that you'll spend some time together – either on a tour or sharing a meal - ask them for their story. Everyone has a story but how often do people get to tell it? People love it and open up. You'll learn about where they live, their culture, the economy of their country, people's expectations from life, their value system, the politics... You'll learn so much and you'll both have a great time.

The Chili Cheese Omelet Opener

When going to a restaurant, I typically eat at the bar or at a communal table. This presents the perfect opportunity for what I now call the Chili Cheese Omelet Opener.

It's simple.

1. Ask the person next to you if they are local. (This immediately tells them that you're not, which also makes you a bit exotic.)

2. Ask if they've been to the restaurant before. If the answer is yes (and you can usually spot a regular) you are set for the last question:

3. "Why don't you order for me?"

Their first response is usually a laugh. People don't believe that I'm sincere. Then they get into it. They take pride in sharing what they think is special about the restaurant, their neighborhood, their city...

I must admit, there are risks associated with this approach. You won't always love what's ordered for you, but connecting with locals makes it worth it.

A Table for One: Restaurants and Meals

Eating alone. Yes, this is one of the biggest concerns people have when they think about traveling solo. But it needn't be an issue. There are many ways to eat alone and feel fine about it and there are also ways to go to a restaurant alone and end up eating with new friends. Here are a few ideas:

Freelance Hubs: Look for independent coffee shops that are used as alternative offices by freelancers. These are places of community. They have a good vibe, they tend to be off the beaten path, they don't rush customers out the door and they usually have free Wi-Fi. They are great places for a light meal.

Restaurants with Communal Tables: Some are casual, some are upscale - there are all kinds of restaurants that have communal tables. You just have to look for them. Communal tables can be great for meeting people, chatting, laughing and learning firsthand about a city or neighborhood.

Restaurants with Bars: Eating at the bar leaves you open for conversation with the bartender if no one else. But I usually do meet other people. In Havana I happened to be reading a very funny book and discovered that when you laugh out loud while reading a book showing an English title, you'll be talking to people in no time.

Pubs or Casual Restaurants: The tables are closer together in these places - great for chatting with people, especially after you've taken a photo of your food. This always attracts attention. A smile in return and a conversation will begin.

Tourist Traps: If you're feeling lonely for home, tourist traps are the places to go. Everyone at these restaurants is from away and many will speak English.

Find Other Solo Diners: Ask the host or hostess whether there is another solo diner who they think would like company or scan the restaurant yourself for a likely person. You can invite them to join you. I haven't been turned down yet.

Picnics: Buy food at a local supermarket or take-out restaurant and eat in a park.

The Classics: Bring a book or write postcards.

Great resource:

Chowhound.com - A community for foodies with discussions sorted by location. This is a great resource for finding foodies' favorite restaurants in most major cities.

Dining Out on Solo Travel Stories

I have had many perks as I've traveled solo. People have gone out of their way to show me their cities. Others have bought me drinks. But in Rochester, New York, I experienced a first.

Leaving my B & B, I went for a wander and to look for a restaurant with a bar where I could have dinner. I found Hogan's Hideaway located on Park Avenue. When I arrived, it was busy but there was one spot at the end of the bar. Sandy and Mark squeezed a bit to let me in and we got chatting.

It's amazing how fast conversations can take off. We talked about their work, my work, travel, travel blogging, and, of course, solo travel. When their table was ready, they invited me to join them. I did and, as usual, I asked Sandy and Mark to order for me. Without hesitation, Sandy ordered a Fish Fry – extra crispy.

Shortly after our meals arrived, so did Tom and Darlene – friends of Sandy and Mark. I continued sharing my solo travel stories but I was more interested in them. Tom had been the owner of the restaurant until a few months before so, when I could, I turned the conversation around and asked about the history of the neighborhood and the restaurant itself.

Tom's father had bought the building as a grocery store in 1948. He and his brothers had delivered groceries by bicycle in their youth. When he took over the business he built a bar onto the back of the store and, eventually, took over the front for the restaurant. My questions kept dragging out more and more history of the place – history that Sandy and Mark didn't know. The climax came when I asked who Hogan of Hogan's Hideaway was. This was great. In North America we think of Hogan as a Gaelic family name. But, in this case, it was the name of the Korean worker who built the bar for Tom – Hó-gan – with the emphasis on the last syllable.

Sandy and Tom were amazed! And it was just as much fun to see their surprise as it was to learn of the history.

The newcomer's advantage is curiosity – I ask questions about things that locals take for granted. The solo traveler's advantage is landing in such wonderful situations with people curious about my stories. Put them together and you too might have the gift of a meal. Sandy and Mark picked up the check for all of us in the end.

How lucky am I?

There is such a thing as a free meal when you travel solo - Rochester, New York, 2010.

 A guide took me to a men's Coffee Shop and taught me to smoke sheesha.
An unusual experience - Aqaba, Jordan, 2011

Evenings with More than a Book

At home, you may not go out alone at night. And, if you do, there are likely a limited number of places that you would go. Maybe a movie is okay but a bar isn't. After all, you have friends to go with and it's uncomfortable to look like you don't.

Traveling solo everything changes. While you don't have those friends as companions, you do have two things on your side:

- Your need to explore the city at night.
- The fact that, as a solo traveler, you are fascinating.

Yes, people will find you interesting simply because you are a traveler and, apparently, an intrepid one at that. So get out there and explore. Great choices for an evening out include:

- Bars with live music.
- Festivals, whether they are cultural, food, music...
- Pubs where the locals hang out.
- Restaurants with communal tables.
- The theater, opera, symphony, ballet.

How to Find the Right Place

I start looking for the right place for evenings before I get into town by reading recommendations on blogs and guides. But I don't assume that I've found it. More than half the time I change my mind after talking to a taxi driver, bartender or server in a restaurant. In other words, I find the best places by talking to locals and being flexible.

Pubbing and Clubbing

You can have a great night on the town alone. I've been to Blues bars, dance clubs, local pubs and, with few exceptions, had a fantastic time meeting people and enjoying the night life. But going out to a club or pub alone successfully requires a slightly different approach than doing so at home with friends. Take these tips:

Getting There

- Don't carry a purse. Leave valuables in the hotel safe or use your money belt for most money, credit cards, passport.... Have some money in different pockets for drinks.
- Dress conservatively for the culture.
- If there's a huge line-up outside a club and you're feeling a bit uneasy about going in alone, find someone in line who looks really safe and approach them as if they are old friends. Then explain that you are alone and would like to join them just until you get inside. They'll understand that you need a bit of safety. Once inside, you can make a graceful exit from them - or you may have made new friends.
- If it's a small place, arrive early so that you have your choice as to where to sit.

Once Inside

- Sit at the bar. It's more social at the bar and you'll be sitting physically higher than most people in the room, giving you a good view for safety.
- Alternatively, choose a seat with a good vantage point. Pubs often have bench seats with tables along two walls. Sit on the short side of this "L" configuration. It's like sitting at the head of a table. You are in a position of power and have access to more people for chatting.
- Make friends with your bartender or server. They'll notice you're alone and take care of you in case of unwanted attention.
- Notice where the exits are. If anything goes wrong you want out fast.
- Choose who you want to talk to and go for it. By being proactive you prevent the wrong person from monopolizing your evening and you'll have a great time with the right people.
- Never drink too much. In fact, drink far less than you would if you were at home. You want to have all your faculties about you to deal with any surprising situations.

Plan Your Exit

- If you have made friends, plan your exit. However nice they may seem, don't accept a ride from them. Get a taxi. This may require leaving early or after them. You can also discreetly ask staff to call you a taxi so that when an offer of a ride does come you have other arrangements.

Dancing in Havana goes on day and night - 2005

Havana, Hungarians and a Salsa Club

A pub, yes. Clubbing, not so much. But I had heard that this one club in Havana was really worth it. So, off I went, not knowing how I was going to manage it.

La Casa de la Música de Centro Habana is one of the city's most popular salsa clubs. It's very large, attracts some of the best bands in the country and hundreds of locals every night. When I went, I saw only three obvious tourists in a massive line up — it made the idea of entering the club solo a bit intimidating. So, I approached those tourists as if they were long lost friends and joined the line.

Unfortunately, my new companions were Hungarian. They barely spoke a word of English. Fortunately, they eventually understood that I was on my own and wanted to join them — at least until I got in the door and sussed out the situation. They were quite accommodating.

Inside, I decided to stick with them despite the language barrier. I still wasn't comfortable. And then I had the greatest of luck. Their local tour guide caught up with them. Exhausted from a day of strained communication, he practically leapt across the table when he realized that I spoke English.

We had a great night. The band was fabulous. The dance floor was a spectacle. And the guide taught me how to salsa.

Sex and the Solo Traveler

Some people wouldn't consider having sex with someone they've just met, but others would. While I don't recommend it, I would like to address the topic.

First the cautionary notes:

- You don't know a stranger. And anyone you've just met – whether it's been an hour, a day or a bit longer – is a stranger. You don't know their values. You don't know their motives. Even if all seems great, they could be playing you. By finding a private place for sex you are putting yourself in danger.

- Whether you speak the language or not, you are in another culture and you won't be able to read the behavior of that enticing person properly. You are out of your element. Assume that your judgment is poor.

- You have no back up – no friends in the area or family to call. You have no one who knows this person to confirm that they are safe.

- Disease contracted through sex is a souvenir you don't want.

It may not be much fun but it is likely a good idea: learn how to say no. Abstinence is definitely the safest choice! But, if after assessing the situation with a somewhat clear head, and within the cautionary notes above, you decide to go for it, please do so safely. Here are a few safety tips:

- Let someone responsible know where you are going. Don't be shy. Text a friend or tell the desk clerk. And let your prospective partner be aware that you are doing so. There is nothing like being seen to increase safety.

- Be aware of the diseases you can contract sexually including:
  - HIV/AIDS, which is transmitted both sexually and via blood
  - hepatitis B, which is also a sexually and blood transmitted disease
  - gonorrhea
  - syphilis
  - herpes
  - chlamydia
  - warts
  - mouth cancer, which has recently been linked to oral sex due to the human papillomavirus.
- Consider being vaccinated for hepatitis A and B as well as the human papillomavirus (HPV) which causes conditions such as genital warts and cancer.
- Practice safe sex. Always use condoms – take condoms from home so that you know they are of good quality.
- If you have exposed yourself to unsafe sex, women should take a pregnancy test. Everyone should go to a clinic to be tested for disease.

Temptation! Yes, it can be tempting sometimes to get involved with someone when traveling, but for the sake of your health and your life, it is advisable to play safe.

Solo Road Trips

I love road trips! Driving music, the open road and the opportunity to change the itinerary on a moment's notice are wonderful. But going solo there are a few details that need your attention.

Make sure you have:

- Roadside assistance - Have a membership to AAA, CAA or some other roadside assistance program.
- A cell phone with good coverage and an adapter so that you can charge it in the car.
- Emergency safety kit that has some food that doesn't spoil, distilled water, blanket, first aid kit, beeswax candle, matches, wind-up flashlight, a whistle and flares.
- GPS – It's not always accurate on highways but, in the city it can be exceptionally helpful - especially with one-way streets.
- A good map – Since a GPS isn't always right and you may want to deviate from its preferred route, it's good to have a map.
- A compass – I find that, despite having a pretty good sense of direction, I sometimes get nervous that I have gone too far, missed an exit or simply took the wrong ramp. A compass is useful as it lets you know that you're at least going in the right direction.
- Your tongue in your mouth – Whenever I was late with a lame excuse, my mother would say "you have a tongue in your mouth, don't you?" The ability to ask questions is essential on any road trip.

My bike fits into the back of my little car for road trips wth a cycling option - Kingston, Ontario, 2010

 Taking a break from the Sundance Film Festival to go skiing at
The Canyons - Park City, Utah, 2010.

Travel Solo for a Rocky Mountain High

It was a stunning day in Park City, Utah. Perfect for skiing. Unfortunately, my day got turned upside down. I had planned to be on the slopes at 9 am but a meeting got in the way and I didn't make it until noon. "Okay," I thought. "I can get in a run or two before heading to town to catch a couple of films." Ah, but fate had other plans. Good plans.

Being mid-week and during the Sundance Film Festival, the ski hill was not busy at all. The sky was an incredible blue. The air was crisp but not chilling. It was a cozy cold. Cold enough to keep the snow dry and your face warm. Going up the gondola by myself I felt full of joy. I actually laughed out loud with delight. This was different from the pleasure of seeing interesting films. This was exhilarating. This was fun.

Given how little time I had, I thought I wouldn't eat but, another couple thousand feet in altitude made me think twice. I headed into the Red Pine Lodge at the top of the gondola to grab a bit of lunch.

In the cafeteria line-up I had a few passing words with a man named Philip. We went in different directions and then met again at the checkout. While the cashier made the suggestion, we decided it was a bit early in our relationship for him to buy me lunch.

We met again at the condiments counter and, as we both scanned the sea of people to find a table, we decided to eat lunch together. Lunch turned into an afternoon of skiing. And what an afternoon!

Philip was a much better skier than me. Fortunately, he was a patient man. He politely took all blue square runs (my comfort level) and skied up the sides and through the trees when the opportunity presented itself. If we were sure that a black diamond and a blue square connected, he took the former and we met at the bottom.

He had the map and, I suspect, he studied it while he waited for me. He guided us run after run so that we never covered one twice. It was fantastic!

And our timing was perfect too. The lifts closed at 4pm and we climbed on for the last ride up at 3:57. We skied all the way to the base getting in every possible skiing minute we could.

What a fantastic day!

Long-Term Solo Travel

Traveling for an extended period of time uses many of the same skills as short solo trips but it does warrant some special attention. You will need to go at a slower pace. You can't travel with the same intensity for a few months as you do for a couple of weeks. This is good because you'll get to know the places you visit on a deeper level.

When planning a long-term trip, consider:

- Regular communication. You may not focus on connecting with home when you're traveling for a short time but on a long trip this will mean a lot to you. Plus, for safety sake, someone should always be aware of your next move. Skype is free with a computer or smart phone and Internet access.
- Renting an apartment on occasion to help you feel more settled. It can also make economic sense.
- Building something into your routine that is familiar to you – something you typically do at home. It could be painting, reading, cooking...
- Using the local library. There may be an English section. You may even be able to get a card.
- Going to the same coffee shop, market or restaurant a number of times to get to know a few of the locals.
- Treating yourself with a small bouquet of flowers or a spa day or a fine scotch. Do something special just for you.
- Exploring the expat situation or meet-up.com as a way to make friends.
- Taking a job. Google "travel jobs abroad" for websites with some unique opportunities for travelers.
- How you're going to manage your money. It may be helpful to have a trusted friend or family member at home to take care of your bills and move money around when necessary.
- A healthy lifestyle. Eat well, drink lots of water... covering all the basics of a healthy lifestyle is more important on long trips than short.
- Picking up a tour and letting someone else take care of all the travel details for a while.

- Taking the train or bus so that you see the countryside and really get a sense of the geography.
- Importing some comfort food. Email home and ask for a care package of your favorite cereal or cookies that you haven't had for a while.
- Inviting friends to join you for periods of time.
- Joining a local running, wine tasting or reading group.

Great resources:

CareerBreakSecrets.com - An inspiring career break blog offering lots of long term travel tips plus great video travel guides specifically designed for long term trips.

MeetPlanGo.com - Annual meetings in major cities across North America to inspire long term travel and answer questions of those wanting to go, plus Career Break Basic Training, an online travel course and community.

Finding Solitude When You Want It

It's probably clear by now that I really like meeting people when I travel. However, some solo travelers go alone to be alone. They are looking for solitude and it can be hard to find.

Here are a few ideas to stave off helpful advice and kind invitations. Here's how to find solitude when traveling solo:

- Go places where solitude is respected – parks, galleries, museums and libraries.
- Look lost in your own thoughts.
- Don't make eye contact with people.
- Dress weird. If you're odd, people are unlikely to approach you.
- Act a little strange — but not strange enough that people offer help.
- Act capable and confident.
- Turn your back to the room in coffee shops and restaurants.
- On a tour, sit in the middle of the bus. Enthusiasts are at the front, people making their own party are at the back.
- Absorb yourself in a book or your diary. If you prefer sketching you may need to employ some of the techniques above as people often feel free to have a look.
- Look grumpy.
- Have the confidence to say that you want to be alone.

I find many opportunities for a little solitude - Lago Todos los Santos,
The Lake District, Chile, 2011

Sharing the Moment

On the flip side of finding solitude is finding ways to share special travel moments so that you don't feel so alone. There are so many ways to do this:

Find a temporary travel mate. Whether for a couple of hours or a few days, solo travelers connect with temporary travel mates all the time. You can meet them at hostels or B & Bs. It's a great way to share travels without a long term commitment. If you've rented a car, others may be willing to chip in on the cost and share the adventure.

Use your smart phone. Sending photos to friends at home at the moment they are taken and chatting by Skype make sharing an experience possible.

Join a short-term tour. Whether it's a one hour tour of a museum or a weekend rafting, you can join a group and share the experience with others – then say ta-ta.

Engage the people around you spontaneously. Take a picture of your food, notice the fantastic desert at the table beside you and smile at the person about to eat it, make an off-hand comment... there are many ways to start a conversation.

Write a personal travel blog. Writing a travel blog to share with friends and family is free and easy.

Master the art of the self-portrait. Don't forget to take photos of yourself on your travels. Sharing these photos when you return tends to open more chances to share your travel experiences than scenery shots. Use the timer or face detection features on your camera. Or just hold it up, point and shoot.

Play with social media. Use Facebook and Twitter to share your experiences in quick, easy and frequent snippets.

Offer yourself as a photographer. Ask someone taking a picture if they would like you to take it for them. Then ask for the favor returned.

Great resource:

TravelBlog.org and TravelPod.com -
both offer free personal travel blogs or interactive journals.

Home is Where Your Heart Is

Over the years, my husband and I traveled many places, just the two of us at times, other times with the kids. Traveling together, we often fell in love with the places we visited. We could imagine living there. We would consider living there. From Saskatoon to the south of France, from California to Scotland, this happened.

One morning on a solo trip around Lake Ontario, I woke up in Prince Edward County. This is an absolutely wonderful place. It has fine wine, fantastic food and great art, along with a rolling landscape, country roads, lake views and beaches. This is a place where my husband and I would have considered living.

At that moment I realized, without him, I was not considering this. It had been possible to think about living elsewhere because I used to travel with my heart; the primary love of my life was with me. Home could be anywhere we were together.

But now that's not the case. I travel solo and the love in my life resides in Toronto where three of my children live, my Mom and my siblings and their families, friends and neighbors — it is these people who now collectively hold my heart.

They are my home.

Safety Trumps Everything

It's simple: safety does trump everything.

This section looks at preventive safety strategies - ways to help you avoid dangerous situations and people. Please read it carefully but keep in mind that it is impossible to cover every situation and circumstance you will encounter. Your safety is ultimately up to you.

Caught in a Con Game in Paris

This is a story of firsts. My first time in Europe. My first solo travel adventure. And my first – and last – time being caught in a con game. It was 1985, I was 27 and I really should have known better.

My trip began in Paris where I spent my time bopping around the city with fellow hostellers – men and women. I felt safe and confident. On the day I was to leave for Salzburg, I felt the same way. I was to take an afternoon train so I stored my backpack in a locker at the Gare de L'est station around noon, then went across the street to look over a menu outside a restaurant. A man approached and checked it out as well. We chatted and went in to spend lunch together. No big deal. Meeting and hanging out with people in Paris seemed normal at this point.

While we were eating, a man at another table leaned over and asked for a light for his cigarette. The fellow I was with (let's call him John) provided it and we all got chatting. It turned out that we were all heading to different cities in Austria.

The other man (I'll call him Peter) got up to leave and casually mentioned that he had to pop into a bank to pick up the Austrian Schillings required to enter Austria. This was before Euros and was news to me. Assuming that this was a detail I missed, I joined the two men and went to get my money changed.

The bank we went to couldn't change our money. It is only with hindsight that I realize that it was likely a commercial bank. I didn't even know of their existence then. From this point on, my life took a very dangerous trajectory that fortunately ended well. My choices at each step may suggest that I am a stupid woman but I'm not. I was, however, very naive.

A con game is all about gaining the confidence of the mark – in this case, me. The end objective is different with every con artist but the process is pretty well the same: prey on a human frailty such as vanity, greed or naivety, gain the person's confidence, then get what you want from them. The thrill of the con is often as important as the results.

After being unsuccessful at the bank, the three of us set out for an Austrian restaurant which John knew. He was sure that the owner would exchange our money so that we could continue our travels. We positioned ourselves at a café across the street from the restaurant. I went to the restroom and took money out of my money belt, went back to the table and gave it to him. Peter gave him cash as well.

As John entered the restaurant across the street, Peter asked how long we had been traveling together. To his apparent shock, I said we weren't travel mates – that I had just met him.

"But, you're my insurance," he said.

We both sat back and waited anxiously to see if our money was lost. However, John returned, explained that he had not been successful and gave our money back.

Confidence earned.

We then went to another Austrian restaurant on the Champs Elysees and repeated the process. This time John returned with Peter's money exchanged but there had not been enough for both of us. Again, he gave me back my money.

Confidence confirmed.

Peter wished us luck and continued on his way. John and I then headed for the Left Bank where we would try once again. I know. You're thinking how crazy I was but it actually seemed pretty realistic. They were pros!

The day was getting on. This time when John went to get the money exchanged he returned and said he had to leave it at the restaurant, but that we could return in an hour to get it. Naturally this made me anxious but there was little I could do. We went for dinner across the street to wait it out.

At dinner John mentioned that we had missed the train and would have to stay overnight; we could share a room. At this proposal I certainly drew the line. I refused and he got angry. When I moved to leave he settled down. After doing this dance a couple of times, I pulled out a photo of my two-year-old son. He looked at me stunned.

"How old are you?"

It was not a good scene. I left him and looked for a phone booth to call a remote connection I had in the city. The booth was occupied. I knocked. I got the one minute hand signal and the person's back. I looked and saw John watching me. I went to the other side of the booth and pounded on it furiously. The man eventually left in a huff and I called. Once it was clear that I was talking to someone I knew, John took off – with my money, of course.

Long story short, I grabbed a cab and went to my contact's home. She said that had John been successful, I would have been en route for the white slave market. Is that the case? I'm not sure. But I certainly wasn't going on any holiday.

The details of that day are indelibly marked in my memory. What saved me was the fact that I stayed in a public place. While I was significantly poorer in the end, I was left with my life – and a lifelong principle for solo travel: public is always safer than private.

That trip lasted another 7 days. I crisscrossed Europe by train as far as Budapest in the east and Amsterdam to the north, and many points in between. As I did, I told the story to as many women as possible.

Travel with the Wit of an Adult and the Wonder of a Child

In 2007, Joshua Bell, one of America's most amazing violinists, played in the subway in Washington D.C. on a violin handcrafted by Antonio Stradivari in 1713 - an instrument that Bell bought several years earlier for a reported $3.5 million.

He was almost completely ignored by the passersby. People pay dearly to attend one of his concerts, yet few stopped to enjoy his beautiful music.

For safety's sake, travel with your wits about you. But also let your guard down at times. Tap into the wonder you had as a child when you knew immediately whether you liked or disliked something. You didn't need a price tag to tell you what you valued then, and you shouldn't now.

(Watch the viedeo)
Watch the video of Joshua Bell here: http://www.youtube.com/watch?v=hnOPuO_YWhw

Janice Waugh

The Four Priorities of Safety

What matters:

Your person.

Your documents.

Your money.

Your stuff.

In that order.

The Five Principles of Safety

When I traveled solo in my twenties, I was on autopilot. I did what came naturally and, with a bit of luck, it all worked out.

Now, as a more mature adult and a blogger, I take time to reflect on what I do and how I do it. When I was asked by another blogger to come up with just five tips for solo travel safety, I struggled. So I came up with five principles - five fundamentals - instead.

If you remember none of the tips that follow this section, I hope that you will remember these five principles.

Solo Travel Principle #1 – Public is safer than private.
This is my number one rule: stay in busy, public places. Regardless of how comfortable you are with a new acquaintance, going to a private place with them can put you in a dangerous situation. Even a taxi should be considered private as you don't necessarily know whether the driver and the acquaintance are friends. So think of public as truly public - where you have control over where you move.

Solo Travel Principle #2 – Proactive is better than reactive.
Imagine yourself in a bar or train station. You have a question or you want to meet someone and have a chat. In situations like this it's better to be proactive than reactive because it's more likely that an inappropriate person will choose you than you will choose him or her. Enjoy the unique social opportunities that solo travel presents but do so on your terms and stay safe.

Solo Travel Principle #3 – People can be engaged in your safety.
When you are walking to a destination but no longer sure of your safety, stop and ask directions even if you know the way. People will redirect you if you're headed into an unsafe area. If you go to a nightclub to take in some music, connect with the bartender or a security guard so that they are aware that you're alone. They'll watch out for you and move unwanted attention away. Whenever possible, subtly engage others in your safety.

Solo Travel Principle #4 – Decisions should not be rushed.
The easiest way to be conned or ripped off is to be rushed into a decision. This is a common strategy of people who want to take you for more than they should. It usually starts with introducing new, credible, but inaccurate information that requires you to make a decision quickly. Don't. Get yourself in a safe place to decide on your terms.

Solo Travel Principle #5 – Being rude can offer protection.
I am sure that you are typically polite and congenial with everyone you meet. After all, it makes for a happier life. However, when it comes to safety, if polite doesn't work, allow yourself to be rude – especially when traveling solo. Regardless of whether it may hurt someone's feelings or disturb other people, if you have to, be rude to ensure your safety.

One further note:
There is a gender bias around safety. Men are often considered to be more dangerous than women but this is not necessarily true. There are dangerous women who are just as capable of luring you into bad situations as men. Be aware of this.

These principles are important but please read the safety tips as well.

- -

"It is we who nourish the Soul of the World and it will become better or worse as we become better or worse."

From The Alchemist, Paulo Coelho

The Beautiful Children of Jordan

"What's your name?"

"What's your name?"

"Janice."

"Ah, beautiful. Beautiful."

"What's your name?"

"Jasmine."

"Farah."

"Halah."

"Raniyah."

There were so many names and so many beautiful, exuberant, outgoing girls on school excursions to Jerash the day I was there.

They wanted to take my picture. They wanted me to take theirs. They wanted to know my name and for me to know theirs. Mostly, they just wanted to talk to a woman who was obviously a foreigner, practice their English which they start learning in grade one, and have fun!

The children I met in Jerash were open, friendly, confident, curious and boisterous. They freely came up and asked me questions, sometimes bouncing up in front of my face to get my attention in a crowd. I loved it.

One teacher told me that the children were thrilled that I was chatting with them – that other tourists had ignored them earlier in the day. What a shame. In a land with Petra, Wadi Rum, the Red Sea and the Dead Sea - in a country with so much to offer - these children were, without a doubt, a highlight of my trip. Regardless of what a country has for travelers, in my estimation, it is the people that make the trip. Jordan is a destination worth revisiting.

The Children of Jordan were a joy - Jerash, Jordan, 2011 ✈

Sixty Tips for Solo Safety

You can't help it. No matter how you try to blend in, you will give yourself away in many ways - large and small. You are a tourist. And because tourists are marks for some of the less genial of characters, please have a read of these tips. Many are just good common sense but, sometimes, they will offer common sense that you've not considered.

They are organized by the four priorities of safety: your person, your documents, your money and your stuff.

Your Person

Before you Leave

- Choose a destination that is appropriate for your travel experience. If this is your first solo travel adventure, go someplace where you speak the language and the culture is familiar.
- Do your research and know the risks of your destination before you arrive. Check your government's travel advisories. Travel guides are valuable sources of information. The Lonely Planet website includes links to a select list of travel blogs like Solo Traveler and has an active traveler community called Thorn Tree where you can ask your specific travel questions.
- Register with your government as a citizen abroad if you're going far and for a while. You can do this on their website.
- Ensure that your accommodation is in a safe part of town. Check it out on sites like TripAdvisor.com and use Google Maps Street View (if available) to see what the area looks like around your accommodation.
- Know the visa requirements of your destination.
- When booking your transportation, schedule your arrival in a new location early in the day so that you have time to adapt to unexpected situations.
- Study city maps so that you have the lay of the land and are able to walk with confidence.

- If you are a quiet person, before leaving, take some time in your basement or some other appropriate place and practice yelling – loudly. We are trained to keep our voices down in public but there may be a time when you will need it.
- Ensure that your cell phone will work where you're traveling and add important phone numbers like those of your accommodation, emergency contacts, family members (with country codes) and your embassy.
- Buy travel insurance. It's a tedious but important detail.
- Schedule vaccinations if appropriate.

Stay Safe in Public

- Always stay in public. Public is always safer than private.
- Stay in well lit, well traveled places.
- Ask locals and other travelers about the safety of an area or destination. Be proactive and choose who you gather information from.
- Stay in touch with home on a regular basis.
- If you see someone suddenly in need of help, go find help for them. Don't go to their aid alone.
- Never choose a restaurant near a train or bus station where unsavory characters look for vulnerable targets.
- When you see signs telling you to be careful of pickpockets DON'T check for your valuables! It's a common reaction and pickpockets watch for people doing just that around these signs so that they know where to pick.
- Carry the name and address of the place you're staying in the local language on a card.
- Dress and act with modesty. Don't flash jewelry, equipment or gadgets of any kind. What you consider cheap could be worth a lot in another place.
- Watch and learn. Take pause before you walk into a public space or even pick up a tomato at a vegetable stand. You'll avoid going into places you shouldn't tread and discover what good manners are in that culture.
- Be aware of your surroundings, the location of exits, who is near you and landmarks to orient yourself.

- If you're a jogger, check about the safety of your route and know it well before going for a run.
- Walk with confidence. Walk like you absolutely know what you're doing.
- Don't wear earbuds or headphones so that you look distracted. It makes you a mark.
- Let a trusted person know where you are going. Because hotel staff have shift changes, you might also leave a note in your room.
- Be aware of and use official taxis only. Official airport taxis are usually less expensive than regular taxis serving the airport. Rogue taxi drivers will serve in peak periods when it's difficult to get a regular cab, but they will charge you a premium and you don't have the protection of a licensed cab. If in doubt, go to a hotel and ask them to get you a cab. Do a bit of research on taxi etiquette at your destination before you leave. Know whether you can hail a cab and how to tell if a cab is available.
- Download maps of transit systems and study them before you set out so that you don't spend undue time studying them in the subway station. Learn the fare system and buy a transit pass available in most major cities. It will always be easier and safer (and sometimes less expensive) to travel off peak hours.
- Don't get on empty subway cars or ones with only a couple of people on them. Choose the busier cars.
- Ask for a hotel room on an upper floor. Women might ask if there is a women-only floor and get a room there if possible.
- Be aware of the alternative exits.
- When you return at night, ask for an escort to your room if you are nervous.
- Use the security lock.
- Carry a whistle to attract attention if you are in a dangerous situation.

Stay Safe with Strangers (Still in Public)

- Trust your intuition. If a person or place doesn't feel right, leave. Be rude if necessary. Malcolm Gladwell studied the potential of an intuitive response in his book Blink: The Power of Thinking Without Thinking. It is powerful. Listen to your gut.

- Stay sober and well rested so that your intuition and decision making are optimal.
- Keep where you're staying to yourself. Your accommodation should be your safe haven.
- Don't be rushed into making a decision – whether it's a purchase, transportation, accommodation.... If you feel rushed you won't be thinking clearly. Find a way to take pause. You can count to 50, do 60 seconds of mindful meditation or simply think of an image that calms you.
- Adapt to and respect cultural differences – be polite on your host country's terms as well as your own.

Your Documents

- Keep your passport and other important documents in the same, secure place at all times. Your passport may stay on you but your trip insurance may stay in your backpack. Wherever you choose, be consistent throughout the trip, and on all trips, and you will be less likely to lose them.
- Have photocopies of your documents with you and have electronic backups as well. You can scan and email your documents to yourself or use one of a number of online document storage services.

Your Money

- Read the "Managing Money" part of Section 2.
- If you want to carry a purse, it should be one with a long, strong strap. Wear it across your shoulder with the opening against your body. This strategy foiled a scooter bandit in Naples, Italy who got away with nothing.
- Carry small amounts of cash in your wallet but have more available in a more discreet place.
- Consider pre-paid debit cards. Some experts consider them better in terms of protecting your personal information than credit cards.
- Only have one credit card accessible. Store the other in a discreet place.

- Traveler's checks may be a good backup if you lose money and can get to a bank.

Your Stuff

- Lock your room carefully and lock important items in the room safe.
- Choose hostels that offer lockers or secure places for luggage.
- Minimize the number of enticing items you carry.
- Don't wear jewelry or flash expensive technology.
- Know what really matters to you. I have a three point check: my wallet, my passport and my camera. Those are the three things that really matter to me.
- Keep things in the same place all the time to reduce the risk of losing them.
- If you use a daypack, carry it on your front with the opening against your body when in busy areas.
- Use a shopping bag from a local store to minimize the tourist look.
- When you leave your room, leave the TV and a light on if possible and put out the 'do not disturb' sign.

Technology as a Safety Tool

- Load your cell phone with all important numbers at home and at your destination and enable a password lockout function.
- Keep your cell phone handy so that you can call for help if necessary.
- If your phone has a siren, learn how to use it. If not, download one from the iTunes store.
- Download a GPS and a translator to your phone.

A Message to Young Solo Travelers

"When traveling solo, your first responsibility is to be safe. If this means losing your money, missing an opportunity, being rude or acting selfish, you have my blessing."

Walking on the ocean floor at low tide near The Caves restaurant - Bay of Fundy, St. Martins, New Brunswick, Canada

I've had many, many wonderful meals in my travels. This extraordinary seafood chowder was at the Bare Bones Bistro - Bay of Fundy, Parrsboro, Nova Scotia, 2011.

Safe Answers to Common Questions

Some people put up a shield when they travel solo by wearing a wedding ring or carrying a picture of a brother to substitute for a husband. But, I'm a really bad liar. So, instead, I've developed the ability to answer common questions with truthful, vague and safe answers. Here are a few examples...

Where are you staying?

Answer: At a B& B in the _____ district. (The answer is not evasive but not specific. You can also elaborate about how the owner has taken you under their wing.)

Can I drive/walk you to your hotel?

Answer: Thanks but I've already called a cab. (Take a bathroom run and call a cab before new friends are making a move to leave. That way you can honestly express gratitude but not accept the ride - in a private car or taxi you no longer have control.)

Are you really traveling alone?

Answer: Yes and no. I always have someone looking out for me. The hotel concierge/B& B owner is expecting me to check in anytime now. (Give people the impression that should you go missing for a minute, people would know.)

What are you up to this evening?

Answer: I have plans. (To spend the evening without this person, keep your response as vague as that. If you wouldn't mind spending the evening with them, meet in a public place away from your accommodation and return via taxi.)

How old are you? (or some more subtle variation)

Answer: Old enough not to tell you. (ha, ha, ha) (Young and older travelers can be targets for con artists whereas people in their 30s, 40s or 50s are less so. Try to present yourself in this age range.)

People are wonderful...

Truly, very few people warrant all the cautions I suggest. Unfortunately, for the few that do, we must travel carefully.

Recognize Potential Danger

An ounce of prevention...you've heard the adage. In this case, it is really important. Preventing a dangerous situation is far easier than defusing one.

Read the Obvious Red Flags
Being aware of your surroundings and how people are acting is critical to your safety.

- Recognize the signs of a bad area. This is a difficult issue for generalizations because what looks 'bad' at home may be typical in another country. Closed stores, few people, no families wandering around can be indicators of an area you want to leave.
- Watch for signs of an unsavory person: contradictions in their story, difficulty maintaining eye contact or making inappropriate demands.
- Look out for services that don't look legitimate: unofficial accommodation offers, unlicensed taxis or someone offering to change money at a great rate.

Know the Common Scams Before you Travel
Watch out for people:

- Posing as police, showing fake ID and asking to see your wallet for counterfeit currency. Scam.
- Giving you something apparently free and then demanding payment. They can be very difficult to say no to, but you must. They'll demand payment as soon as the item is in your hands.
- Taking your picture for you and then demanding a fee.
- Spilling ice cream, ketchup or coffee on you or causing some other distraction so that their partner can pickpocket you.
- Managing your credit card while on the phone. A cashier doing this may be taking a photo of your card with the phone's camera.

Across Canada By Train

While Canada is known for its expansive territory in the great north, almost 90% of Canadians live within 60 miles of the American border. Canada is essentially an east-west country. Sitting in central Canada planning a spring train trip, I had two choices – go east, or west. With family in Vancouver, I chose west.

For this trip, I chose to travel coach. I did so for two reasons: the price and the people – the latter being the most important. In first class there are many very nice people but in coach, there are really interesting people. On my trip to Vancouver, I spent 3 days (and 3 nights) with the most interesting, entertaining people one could imagine. It started before leaving the station.

The Casket Makers
I boarded the train, organized my stuff, sat down and looked across the aisle. There sat a young teenage boy with a wooden casket for suitcase.

Yes, I thought. This is going to be an interesting trip.

Shortly after we pulled out of the station I could contain myself no longer. "Uh, what's that?" I asked.

The boy was about 13 and still in the sweet boy stage. "It's a model casket," he said. "My Dad and I make pine boxes."

"Ahhh, I said."

When his Dad returned I got the full story. Father and son were from Prince George, British Columbia and makers of simple pine boxes. They had taken the train from Prince George to Toronto to be on the television show, The Dragon's Den – a reality show where you pitch your company to get financing from five successful business people. The pitch hadn't won them any money but it had been an adventure and gained publicity for their company. Having recently experienced far too much death in my family, I had a very interesting discussion with the father.

"The Canadian" goes from Toronto to Vancouver - Via Rail across Canada, 2008 ✈

Burning Man Survivors
The bar car on a train is like a kids' playground. You just have to watch for a bit, wait for an opening and jump in. This may not work in your neighborhood bar, but on the train it's almost expected. There is no established social order. Everyone is traveling. And everyone has a tale to tell.

It was in the bar car that I met a wonderful hippie couple from – well, from nowhere any more. They used to have a home in Manitoba but they sold that and chose travel instead. To have some sort of base they had recently bought a share in a trailer in northern Manitoba. This couple told of their journeys. The one that stands out most in my mind was their experience at Burning Man, an annual art event / temporary community built in the Nevada desert. They were the first people I had ever met who had a firsthand account of this legendary event.

Multicultural Euchre
I like the options that trains offer. When I felt like solitude, I spent time at my seat reading or watching the scenery. When I wanted fun, I just went to the dome car where you could get a better view of the landscape and socialize.

Most people on the train were from various provinces in Canada but I also met people from Korea, France, Germany and Japan. Walking into the dome car at one point, an adult was leaving a kids' game of euchre. They needed a fourth – adults tire of such games faster than kids. I joined in. Four players from three countries. We had a great time.

And Many Others...
In addition to these highlights there was the guy from Israel who told me all about the love of his life, the couple from Newfoundland who had been sleeping side by side for four days en route to see a new grandchild, the retired railroad worker who explained how the train signals worked across the prairies and the fellow from Quebec who was the first of his family to travel outside of the province.

Canada is a spectacular country and traveling by train is a great way to see it. It takes time but it is well worth it.

Happy Trails - Bon Voyage - Safe Travels

Remember the couch I wrote about in the Backstory?

Well, since launching Solo Traveler, my relationship with it has changed dramatically. It is now a place for dreaming, not grieving. When I got up off the couch that Saturday afternoon, my life was different.

Two months later, I launched Solo Traveler. Six weeks after that I was on my first trip as a blogger. Now, two years and many trips later, I find daily joy in the comments left on my blog, in Twitter exchanges and in discussions on a Facebook community ironically named The Solo Travel Society. I enjoy meeting other solo travelers wherever I go and I love speaking about the entire experience to groups.

I've been rehearsing for this role my entire life.
It has been said to me:

> "Yes, it's easy for you. You're an extrovert."

In fact, I'm not. Speak to those who knew me in my teens and twenties and they'll tell you that I was shy. Talk to anyone who was in the audience the one time that I stood at a podium in my thirties and they'll tell you that it was a painful experience for the entire room. No, it's not that I'm outgoing, it's that I'm willing to go out and try. And, the more I've done it, the more experience I've accumulated, the more extraordinary my travel has become.

And now it's your turn.
I think I've shared most of what I wanted to say now. I've given you tips about money and packing, road trips and long term travel, safety and meeting people... While there is much more about solo travel on my blog, really, what's left is for you to go.

Yes, go. Go around the world or around the corner. Go solo and enjoy the people, culture, history, mountain views, seascapes and city skylines. Enjoy adventures and challenges.

But, mostly, go and enjoy how solo travel enriches your life. Discover the world as you discover yourself.

Go and see what you don't know is there.

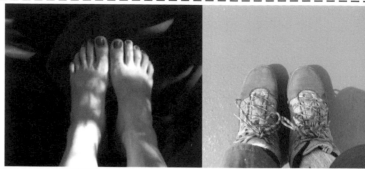

 I take pictures of my feet as I travel. Above (L to R) are my feet in Mexico, Chile, the United States, Jordan, Canada and Spain

Janice Waugh publishes Solo Traveler (solotravelerblog.com), the blog for those who travel alone. She has been quoted in many media outlets including the Washington Post, Chicago Tribune, LA Times and the Toronto Star. In addition to writing, she enjoys speaking to groups about solo travel and was thrilled to be invited to do so at the Smithsonian Institute. Her blog offers solo travel stories, tips, safety advice and destination ideas as well as the free ebook Glad You're Not Here: a solo traveler's manifesto. The Solo Traveler's Handbook is her first published book. Janice has a Masters Degree in History and, when not traveling, she lives in Toronto.

Janice Waugh

Janice Waugh

CPSIA information can be obtained
at www.ICGtesting.com
Printed in the USA
LVIW011429020812
292694LV00001B